ONS

THE
BRIDGES
OF
MADISON COUNTY

Jeffrey Richards   Stacey Mindich   Jerry Frankel

Gutterman Chernoff, Hunter Arnold, Ken Davenport, Carl Daikeler, Michael DeSantis,
Aaron Priest, Libby Adler Mages/Mari Glick Stuart, Scott M. Delman, Independent Presenters Network,
Red Mountain Theatre Company, Caiola Productions, Remmel T. Dickinson, Ken Greiner,
David Lancaster, Bellanca Smigel Rutter, Mark S. Golub & David S. Golub, Will Trice

WITH **Warner Bros Theatre Ventures**

AND **The Shubert Organization**

IN ASSOCIATION WITH **Williamstown Theatre Festival**

PRESENT

Kelli O'Hara   **Steven Pasquale**

• IN •

THE
BRIDGES
OF
MADISON COUNTY
A NEW MUSICAL

BOOK BY   MUSIC & LYRICS BY
Marsha Norman   **Jason Robert Brown**

BASED ON THE NOVEL BY **Robert James Waller**

WITH
Hunter Foster

Michael X. Martin   **Cass Morgan**

Caitlin Kinnunen   **Derek Klena**   **Whitney Bashor**

Ephie Aardema   Jennifer Allen   Charlie Franklin   Kevin Kern   Katie Klaus   Luke Marinkovich
Aaron Ramey   Dan Sharkey   Jessica Vosk   Tim Wright

SCENIC DESIGN	COSTUME DESIGN	LIGHTING DESIGN	SOUND DESIGN
Michael Yeargan	**Catherine Zuber**	**Donald Holder**	**Jon Weston**

HAIR & WIG DESIGN	ORCHESTRATIONS	CASTING	MUSIC COORDINATOR
David Brian Brown	**Jason Robert Brown**	**Telsey + Company** **Abbie Brady Dalton, CSA**	**Michael Keller**

ADVERTISING	PRESS REPRESENTATIVES	PROPS	ASSOCIATE PRODUCERS
Serino/Coyne	**Irene Gandy/Alana Karpoff** **Thomas Raynor/Christopher Pineda**	**Kathy Fabian**	**Steven Strauss** **Michael Crea** **PJ Miller**

TECHNICAL DIRECTOR	PRODUCTION STAGE MANAGER	COMPANY MANAGER	GENERAL MANAGER
Hudson Theatrical Associates	**Jennifer Rae Moore**	**Katrina Elliott**	**101 Productions, Ltd.**

MOVEMENT
Danny Mefford

MUSIC DIRECTOR
Tom Murray

DIRECTION
Bartlett Sher

World premiere production presented in August 2013 by the Williamstown Theatre Festival
Williamstown, Massachusetts, Jenny Gersten, Artistic Director
Presented with the cooperation of Warner Bros. Theatre Ventures, Inc.

The producers wish to express their appreciation to the Theatre Development Fund for its support of this production.

For information on performance rights for *The Bridges of Madison County*
contact Music Theatre International **www.mtishows.com**

ISBN 978-1-4950-0344-8

7777 W. BLUEMOUND RD. P.O. BOX 13819 MILWAUKEE, WI 53213

Visit Hal Leonard Online at
www.halleonard.com

CONTENTS

TO BUILD A HOME

Music and Lyrics by
JASON ROBERT BROWN

14

Grand Waltz

learn to speak, I learn to sew, I

learn to let the long - ing go, The

trac - tor wheel, a foot of snow, I

TEMPORARILY LOST

Music and Lyrics by
JASON ROBERT BROWN

Steadily, but with mystery, in 3 ($\bullet$ = 86)

ROBERT: (conversationally)

I left eight days a-go from Wash - ing-ton.

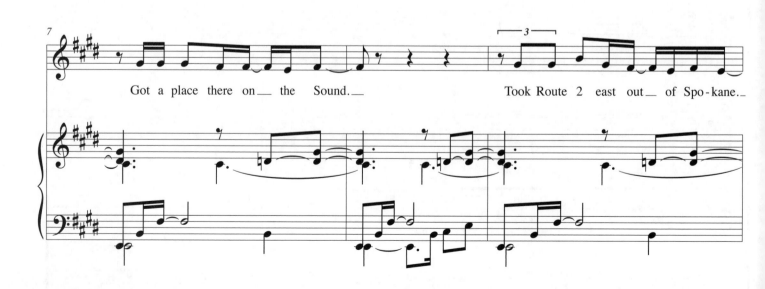

Got a place there on the Sound. Took Route 2 east out of Spo-kane.

WHAT DO YOU CALL A MAN LIKE THAT?

Music and Lyrics by
JASON ROBERT BROWN

Quasi Minuétto

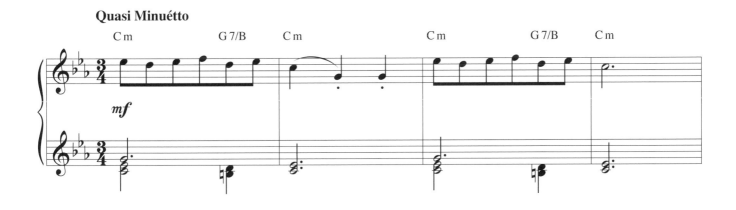

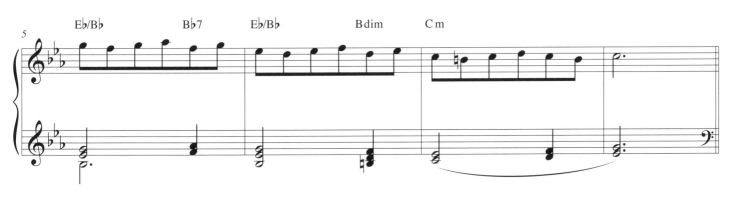

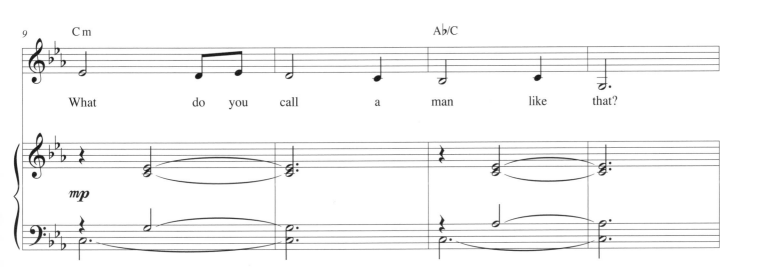

What do you call a man like that?

A tempo
93
C m/E♭
Want - ing some - thing,
mp
97
B♭m/E♭
Know - ing some - thing,
101
C m/E♭
See - ing some - thing,
105
B♭/D
Some - thing ho - ly–

36

ANOTHER LIFE

Music and Lyrics by
JASON ROBERT BROWN

WONDERING

Music and Lyrics by
JASON ROBERT BROWN

Moderato, with stillness ($\bullet$ = 112)

ROBERT:
A lit-tle twinge,_ A lit-tle shock,_ A lit-tle whis-per at the bot-tom of_ your mem-o-ry.

A sud-den wind_ A gen-tle knock,_ And then a rus-tle____ in

THE WORLD INSIDE A FRAME

Music and Lyrics by
JASON ROBERT BROWN

Lightly, in 1 (♩. = 68)

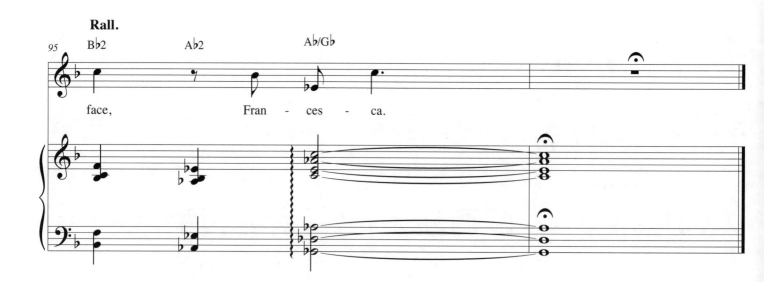

FALLING INTO YOU

Music and Lyrics by
JASON ROBERT BROWN

ALMOST REAL

Music and Lyrics by
JASON ROBERT BROWN

Chaconne, poco rubato, in 1

Rall.

FRANCESCA:

When a

A little faster (♩ = 168)

girl   grows   up   in   Na - po - li,   There   are

143 Fm6/G

end up a farm wife, ex - haust - ed and numb. I'm

147 Eb+ · Rall.

off to the ser - vice - man's club; you should come!" But I

A tempo
151 C

dreamed of the beach at An - co - na, Where our

mp

155 G 7/C

kids would play,_____ Pao - lo

BEFORE AND AFTER YOU/
ONE SECOND AND A MILLION MILES

Music and Lyrics by
JASON ROBERT BROWN

Gently, rolling (♩. = 62)

FRANCESCA:

Hold-ing you close a-gainst my skin, And pull-ing you___ in-side me,

Sud-den-ly there's a world I___ nev-er knew.

WHEN I'M GONE

Music and Lyrics by
JASON ROBERT BROWN

IT ALL FADES AWAY

Music and Lyrics by
JASON ROBERT BROWN

ALWAYS BETTER

Music and Lyrics by
JASON ROBERT BROWN